I0481008

DONE DEAL!™

THE STEP-BY-STEP HANDBOOK
TO SALES SUCCESS

JEFFREY BRANDEIS

DONE DEAL!

THE STEP-BY-STEP HANDBOOK TO SALES SUCCESS

JEFFREY BRANDEIS

Movicorp

MovicorpMedia.com

DONE DEAL! A Step-by-Step Handbook to Sales Success
Copyright ©2020 Jeffrey Brandeis. All rights reserved.

No part of this book may be used or reproduced in any manner
whatsoever without prior written permission of the author except
in the case of brief quotations embodied in critical articles and
reviews.

DONE DEAL! is a trademark of Done Deal Sales Training, a
division of Brandeis Sales Solutions, LLC.

Printed in the United States of America.

Book design by Marilyn Rodriguez, Art in Motion Graphic Design

www.artinmotiononline.com

Project Management

Movicorp

MovicorpMedia.com

Contents

CHAPTER 3 (CONT.)

CHAPTER 4: ALIGN WITH BUYER

CHAPTER 5: DONE DEAL!

Dedication

I would like to thank my wife Jan, my son Daniel and my daughter Megan for putting up with all my travel over the years.

Even though I missed events in all their lives, what I did in pursuing my career was to help provide them a quality of life that I might not have been able to do otherwise. Love you all very much.

Also want to thank all the sales reps and sales leaders that I have worked with and for, as I learned from each of you something that has helped me grow as a person.

And finally a shout-out to you, the readers of this work, I say -- Good Selling!

Jeff Brandeis
Tampa, Florida
September 2020

Prologue

> " Opportunities don't happen. You create them.
> — Chris Grosser, Marketing Executive "

W hether you're a sales representative, sales manager, sales engineer/architect, vice president of sales or even a market support representative, every how-to book you read must help enhance your craft.

DONE DEAL! is a universal sales process I developed to help you gain new and effective techniques to master your craft. And selling, dear reader, is indeed a "craft."

Every company employee is in sales. From customer service, administration, billing, collections, and even the people that clean your office, all have an impact on sales. If you are a sales leader, it's your job to help make your team understand the role they play and their core deliverables.

What you say and how you say it is imperative to closing a successful sale and keeping that customer for many years to come. But more on solid "relationship building" later.

Most sales reps try to take short cuts and usually fail. One big reason is because they are not ahead of their prospects in their buying process, such as how their prospect's process runs and the manner in which they buy. You may ask, "Really? My prospect/buyer has a buying process?" Yes they do. We will get into this further, as well.

Sales is your chosen profession. You are the solution expert who performs the heavy lifting in a sales presentation and, often, the one to close. Much like a medical doctor, an athlete or a hairdresser, you must continue getting better and better at what you do and how you do it.

DONE DEAL! is your next big step toward improving those skills that will have a positive effect on you and your craft. It will take you through the entire sales process, from prospecting all the way to closing the sale. If you follow every step in this process, you will be successful.

Let's get started now!

Chapter 1:
GAINING ACCESS

> Today's knowledge has power. It controls access to opportunity and advancement.
> — Peter Drucker (1909-2005)
> Author and Management Consultant

Getting to the people you need to get to is a lot different today than it was 20, 10, 5 or even one year ago. Technology has changed how businesses operate, how we communicate, how we learn and how we sell. If you are still doing the same things as you did 5 years ago and you are successful, that's great. But very soon you won't be. The selling process is rapidly changing and in many industries it has already transformed completely.

Think about it. Do you buy a computer the same way today that you did a few years ago? A TV? An appliance? I truly doubt it. Today you go on the Internet, you research models, you research features, options, prices. You go on Facebook, you blog, you tweet. You communicate with people you don't even know before you actually step into a showroom or retail store. If you even do that! Many consumers are even buying cars online without stepping into a car dealership.

Today's buyer is more sophisticated than a couple of years ago. They know your company and they know the competition. They know your strengths and weaknesses possibly even better than you do or even your product manager does. Scary, isn't it?

So how do we gain access in today's world? It's not easy, what with caller ID, email security, spam filters, fire walls and, of course, the dreaded administrative assistant who screens all calls, often called the "gatekeeper."

THE COLD CALL

Let's talk about the dreaded cold call. Some sales professionals believe this is no longer part of a sales rep's arsenal. Many believe it's a waste of time. Yet, all of you do it, most managers expect you to do it, and even I expect my sales team to do it.

When the marketing folks provide you lists of new contacts to call, typically called "leads," you are expected to reach out to them as the initial point of contact. More than likely, your company has a dashboard in their CRM (Customer Relations Management) software that tracks your calls, as well. Yet most of you have very little success in this methodology. Why is that? Several reasons, but probably the biggest is because your message and process is no different from that of countless other sales reps doing exactly the same thing.

Let's relate this to your personal life. How many calls do you get at home from someone trying to sell you something? Do you listen to them? Do you buy? Do you even pick up the phone if it's from an unknown number or you don't recognize the caller ID name? My guess is no. And why is that? Because they all sound exactly like you.

Sorry if I just made you upset with me, but you know it's true. In your quest for tutoring to achieve 100% success, nothing I am going to suggest hasn't already been invented. But if you follow what I am going to share with you, and you don't skip steps, it will increase your chances of gaining access to potential buyers.

Ready?

 *Hello Mr./Mrs. ABC, my name is Jeff and I am with XYZ company. Our company is the leading provider of widgets in the US. Our products are the best in the industry and I would like the opportunity to discuss how our products can help you. My number is 555-666-7777. Looking forward to speaking with you. Have a great day.*

Sound familiar? Great voice mail, isn't it? Is this basically your pitch? Close to it? Let's be honest. It stinks – it's a message from a first grader.

THE ELEVATOR PITCH

Imagine you're on the tenth floor of an office building. Elevator doors open and you step in. There's another person in the elevator. Each of you acknowledge each other and nod. And then it happens. He or she asks you what you do. Your answer is probably the same as your voice mail. And when you ask what this stranger does, the response more often than not is exactly like yours, except for the person's name, company and perhaps job title.

And what comes of this so-called "Elevator Pitch?" More often than not, nothing. Nada. Zilch.

Think about it: Was the above voice mail message compelling? Was there a call to action? Does it differentiate you in any way versus. the competition or their current vendor? Does it show that you know anything - and I mean anything - about their business? Probably No, No! and NO!

So what exactly should be in your elevator pitch or in your voice mail?

Both should contain 3 things:

- Let the prospect quickly understand your business' product or service
- Let the prospect know what your product or service can do for them
- Keep it Short & Sweet, never more than 20–30 seconds

Your pitch also should be:

- Interesting, memorable, and succinct.
- Crystal-clear as to what makes you – or your company, service or product – unique.

A compelling voice mail, email or elevator pitch also must contain:

- Your name, company & product name
- The Benefit, meaning the reason(s) your prospect might want or need what you're selling
- The Differentiator, meaning the reason(s) your prospect should buy from you instead of your competition
- Engage with a Question, meaning you ask for a phone or in-person meeting

If you can do this, the probability of getting a return phone call or email will increase substantially. For example:

Hello, companies like Prospect's Company turn to me/us to solve their day-to-day legal challenges. I'm with AB Company, and we have software that solves three of your greatest challenges: (1) Actionable data insights which (2) increases visibility into your company's performance, and (3) that answers the question, "Can I litigate fewer claims and improve expense ratios?" My name is Jeff Brandeis and if those areas concern you, I can set up a time to talk more about how we can help your company. My number is xxx-xxx-xxxx.

Would you be intrigued enough to call me back? Who knows, but far more likely than the first example. Let's try another one:

Companies like yours (or insert company name) come to me/us (or insert company name) when they're trying to control the pressures of expense or loss ratios and gain insight into their overall performance. This is done using our patented platform with support tools designed to streamline work and give actionable data, aiding in decision making. Would you like to grab coffee and discuss? My name is Jeff Brandeis, and my number is xxx-xxx-xxxx.

Far more insightful and powerful, the above provides your prospects with something tangible about your product and your company.

So begin by writing out a few different versions. Try them out to find the ones that work for you. No single pitch will fit all of your needs or situations. For verbal pitches (live or voice mail recordings), the more you practice, the smoother and easier you will be able to say them. For both verbal and written (email) pitches, the more you use them, the more likely you will tweak, refine and improve it, as well. It's all good as long as you remember the key points:

- Let the prospect quickly understand your business' product or service

- Let the prospect know what your product or service can do for them

- Keep it Short & Sweet, never more than 20–30 seconds

Let's move along now…

You left a voice mail and/or emailed your prospect and have gotten no response. Do you give up? Most sales reps do. The super sales reps do not. Successful reps often tell me it will take 7 to 12 "touches" before a prospect returns an email or voice mail. And why shouldn't it? You need to earn your way in, you need to build credibility, you need to become a reliable resource. Your buyer needs to know you know his business, you know your industry and what you are sharing with him/her is valuable. This takes time, this takes patience.

MIXING IT UP

Successful sales reps mix up how they reach out to a prospect. Mix up? What does that mean? Change my voice mail? Change my email? Not at all.

The definition of insanity is doing the same thing over and over again and expecting different results. If you keep sending the same email or leaving the same voice mail with no success, why do you continue doing it? Probably because your sales manager is telling you to, your marketing department is telling you to - or you just don't know any better.

What I am suggesting is that you "mix up" both the content and style of your messaging so that each time you reach out to someone, he or she receives something completely different from your prior communications. It tells your prospects you're truly interested in them and willing to invest the time and resources to meet with them.

Ultimately, your imagination and initiative will determine the mix up strategies that work best for you. For now, below are a few mix up strategies that have proven successful over time.

Create your own personalized, customized video. Video? Are you serious? I want you to video record yourself? Yes, I do. We have had pretty good success in getting a response back from a prospect using video, especially ones that have ignored us in the past. The cost is minimal, if anything at all. Your video should not be longer than 90 seconds, if even that long. You can use a video camera or your smartphone to do this. Always begin your video by introducing yourself and your company. Depending on your particular product or service, and the market you're trying to reach, the camera can be mounted on a tripod or selfie stick. You can be seated, standing, even walking -- but the image must be in focus, well lit and your voice clear and at a healthy volume.

Oh, and wear something very nice that shows you're a professional.

Your message must be compelling and provide something useful to your prospect. For example, tell them about a white paper your company created that would be of tremendous value to them. Don't ask for a meeting, just provide them with value. If you can create a series of videos (say, one per week), they likely will ask you for a meeting - or they will take your call. But they must believe you are providing them with something they are not getting elsewhere.

If you have a marketing department, ask them to upgrade your video by adding a company border or logo. On-screen graphics. Maybe even music. You might be surprised what the folks in marketing can do. If not, do this on your own.

One of my software sales reps took this concept and incorporated his love for hockey. He had his aunt film him on the ice. He was dressed in a suit and tie, he had his hockey stick along with a puck and he skated up to the camera. His pitch talked about playing for the state championship in that same arena and how having the proper tools and the right game plan that led to success on the ice is no different than having the right software (or other product) for your company. The software should help show area of risks and opportunities for improvement. Everything that his coach did for him and his team, his company's software will do for the prospect watching the video. WOW! Isn't that compelling? Isn't that different? Would this get your attention? I wish I could say he received hundreds of calls, but he didn't. However, he did get a 9% response rate which any marketing person will tell you is truly outstanding. Sales reps would be ecstatic with this type of result.

In today's competitive sales game, differentiating yourself from the competition will at least get you in the door. From there it becomes more about your sales skills, your product and your team. So you must constantly be thinking of how to set yourself apart from the pack by doing things differently, by mixing things up.

 ## TIMING YOUR OUTREACH

There are many online communication tools available today. New programs, SASs and apps seem to appear daily. Regardless of which tools you use, the next question is frequency. How often should you communicate with a new prospect? You must be diligent, but not desperate. You want to appear confident, but not a pest.

The following chart sets forth a sample time frame for reaching out to new prospects. It utilizes email, ClearSlide and Sidekick apps, but any tool can work if you follow a well-planned strategy.

SAMPLE OUTREACH SCHEDULE

ATTEMPT	SUGGESTED TIME FRAME	HOW	WHAT
1	Day 1	Email using a program that can track if email was opened	Email message - introduction and setting stage for future correspondence
2	7 days later	Email	Attach or include White Paper #1 that provides value to your prospect
3	7 days later	Hard copy mail	White Paper #2 that provides additional value to your prospect with handwritten cover note
4	7-10 days later	Phone	"Hope you've been finding value in the materials sent so far" – Provide heads-up on presentation link they will receive
5	3-7 days later	Tracking email	Email presentation link with invitation to attend

SAMPLE OUTREACH SCHEDULE (cont)

ATTEMPT	SUGGESTED TIME FRAME	HOW	WHAT
6	3 days later	Mail	Product Sheet with message of how customers are using the product in various ways - Cover Letter, Product Sheet, and Company notepad or other trade show giveaway branded with your logo
7	6 days later	Mail Printed Invitation using Company Notecards OR send invite by email	Invitation to schedule 20-minute review w/ attached PPT (PowerPoint) or say that "I'll go away."
8	7-10 days later	Email	Confirm Yes/No on Invitation to review/discuss PPT

SAMPLE OUTREACH SCHEDULE (cont)

ATTEMPT	SUGGESTED TIME FRAME	HOW	WHAT
9	3 days later	Package by mail	White Paper #3 - " again providing value to your prospect (can be used either way - if they have no interest in PPT or as follow-up to the PPT discussion)
10	10 days later	Tracking email	"Wishing you all the best" PLUS one of 2 options – "Thanks anyway. If your needs change in the future, please call me" OR if timing isn't right: "Will check back in a few months."

WORKING WITH LINKEDIN

Another highly-effective strategy for providing value to both current and potential customers is utilizing LinkedIn – the Facebook for business professionals.

So get busy joining and creating affinity groups and reach out to buyers to connect with you.. Post articles, written by you or others, that prospects and your current customers can use.

"But how do I get people to join my group?" is what I hear my reps ask me. "My company won't pay for the higher levels of memberships." Obviously, you can invest your own money and do this. Maybe – just maybe – if you are successful and show your company the ROI (Return On Investment), they might cover the monthly expense to upgrade your LinkedIn membership.

If neither you nor your company is willing to pay to upgrade your membership, try this. Invite an unresponsive prospect to connect with you via a LinkedIn invitation. Tell him or her in the invitation message that "While you don't know me, please accept my invitation so I can share valuable information that will help you and your company."

We have seen a very high rate of acceptances to this method. This is not about your products or you telling them how wonderful your company is and that you provide the best service in the industry -- who cares?

They don't, and neither should you. At this stage, it's all about making a connection. Gaining access. If you don't establish a connection, the rest is immaterial. Make sense? Of course, not everyone will accept your invitation, but of those that do so, it's now up to you to deliver value by providing concepts, ideas and articles that, hopefully, they have not seen or thought of before.

 ## CURRENT CUSTOMERS = BEST SALES AGENT

The greatest short-cut to growing your sales is through referrals. And who better to provide them than your current customers. They talk to contemporaries in similar positions at other companies, they attend conferences and conventions. In short, they network. Which makes them your best sales agent, assuming, of course, they are happy customers.

How many of you ever ask your customers for a referral? Or if they know someone at a different company? Provide value to this group and your customers will forward your information to coworkers; they might even forward your information to a prospect. If you do this right, you soon may discover people joining your group that you don't even know! How cool would that be? Even more exciting is when one of these new people ask you to come in and talk about your company, talk about your product or service. That is for what we all hope and strive.

The good news is that it can happen to you if you willing to put in the work.

BOOSTING EMAIL/ VOICE MAIL RESPONSE RATES

Put yourself in the buyer's shoes. What gets you to respond to an email? What makes you respond to a voice mail?

Most of us receive a voice mail, listen to it for maybe a second or two and then delete it. Why not take a few of the voice mails you receive from others and critique them. First, write them down word-for-word. What do you like about them? What don't you like about them? What if you took the good parts of several voice mails and combined them into one and made it your own? Hmmm, bet you never thought about that before.

Don't use their words verbatim, use your own words. When you do come up with a voice mail script, make sure you practice it until you have it memorized so as not to sound like you're reading it. That alone can turn off a prospect and result in the dreaded delete.

I can usually tell when reps are reading versus just speaking naturally, especially over webinars. It's just something in the tone, their manner that says to me they are reading vs talking naturally..

Again, nothing here is revolutionary or brand new. But hopefully you've gained a few ideas new to you and you've begun to think more about what you can change or try that could lead to greater success in gaining access.

So let's move along now and assume you have gained access to speak to your prospect. You are on the phone with him/her. Now what? What I see more often than not is the sales rep goes into what his/her company is all about and how great their product is. They talk and they talk and they talk. Again, as I said earlier regarding your compelling voice mail or elevator pitch, your first real conversation with your prospect should be geared towards them - not all about you. Yes, you want them to know your name and what your company does. But beyond that, wait until your prospects tell you something about themselves and their company.

How different would this be?

 *Hello Susan, I appreciate you taking my call. My name is Jeff Brandeis and I am with ABC company. But before I tell you more about my company, can you tell me about what you do and what tools you use today to accomplish your objectives?*

Different? Probably. Will Susan tell you? Maybe, maybe not. But what you do is try to make this conversation about her and her company -- not about you. In my mind, you have not yet earned the right to talk about the things you do. Most people like to talk about themselves but, unfortunately, most sales representatives don't allow their prospects or customers talk. Why is that? Because you are too busy talking about yourself! Have you ever heard the expression, "You were born with two ears and one mouth?" You should listen twice as much as you talk, but most sales reps don't.

If you are successful in getting Susan to talk about herself, her job, what tools she is using today and perhaps some of her challenges as well, you will be much better prepared to answer her needs by custom-tailoring what your company does that can make her more successful or her company more profitable. Do not blindly talk about your products or services that Susan might not care about. By having her talk about herself first, you then can modify and mold your conversation around her, thus making your pitch a lot more compelling to her.

You're now thinking, "This is so obvious, why did Jeff even bother to write it?" Because most of you don't do this, most of you dive into your product, your company, how you have the best, most unique software, widget or whatever, and how you have helped companies like Susan's.

How on earth, though, can you say this with confidence when you have no idea what Susan is all about?

As an example, I enjoy going car-shopping with my daughter and I just love it when the car sales person says to me, "What will it take to get you into this car today?" Since I'm a New Yorker (sorry for stereotyping here, no offense but...) I am a self-confessed wise guy. My answer is always, "Take my trade-in and give me the keys to my new car."

Obviously the sales reps looks at me like the wise guy I am and repeats to me more seriously, "What will it take?" I look back and say, "I just told you." They usually reply, "You know I can't do that." "Yes, I know, but you asked a question and I gave you my answer. Now do you want to understand more about me and my needs versus how you're going sell a car right this second?"

This back-and-forth truly happened more than once, leaving my daughter laughing hysterically. Obviously we didn't buy a car that day, nor returned to that dealership ever again. People usually don't like high-pressure sales people. Especially today, when it's possible customers know more about the cars they want than the sales person.

Another suggestion here is don't just do small talk for the sake of small talk and then turn up the pressure or the heat. Take your time, invest in your prospect, invest in your customers. Learn from them, let them teach you. The more you learn from them. the better positioned you will be to close more sales.

OK, now back to Susan. You've asked her about her role in the company, her responsibilities, what tools she uses today that makes her successful. Most reps then go for broke and ask about her biggest challenges. Sometimes Susan might tell you, but I suggest you first ask, "What do you really like most about your current product or service?" If she tells you she is not happy with it, you could be on your way to gaining greater access and a sale. But if she tells you that she is happy – well, what do you say now? "What are your biggest challenges?" She replies "None." Then what? Is adios, au revoir or goodbye next?

No! Try following up with this: "Susan, I think it's great you're happy with your current provider. But like all programs/products/services, there are always a couple of enhancements you would love to see them make. May I ask you what those would be?"

What did I just do? Oh my, I told Susan that I was glad she was happy with her vendor. Why would I do that? Why wouldn't you? Are you going to tell her that her current vendor is bad? That they have terrible software? Where do you think that will get you?

What I did was compliment her on her current choice of vendor, but I also asked what her enhancement requests are. Why did I do that? To gain trust is one reason. Of course, I'm hoping that her enhancement requests are something that my company already provides, which would be an immediate benefit to her.

But what if we don't, or I don't know if we can or cannot? Then acknowledge that those are great enhancements. If your company does provide them, ask if you could show this to her. If you're not sure, or know your company does not provide those enhancements, ask if you can check internally and give her a call back with an answer. Susan should say sure no problem.

But before you say goodbye, ask her what other challenges she or her co workers face . For these "items," your products and/or services deliver proven solutions that she isn't getting today or possibly even thinking about just yet.

This is where you differentiate yourself from other sales reps. This isn't about you. It's about the prospect. It's about providing value that your competitor isn't providing. It's about winning. This might be your only opportunity to speak with Susan. If you are not compelling, if you don't bring value to her, why would she ever speak to you again? Would you speak to a sales rep that brought no value? No, that would be a waste of time. Why would you expect her to be any different?

Let's go back to one of the enhancements that Susan wants. You don't have it today but it's on the road map to be released in six months or a year. What then? You call her back and tell her. More than likely her response will go something like this: "That's great to know, Jeff, please let me know when you do have it and we can talk then."

A blow off ? Perhaps, yes. Most reps will reply, "It sounds good, I will make a note and call you back when we have it." You hang up feeling good that you have a prospect lined up for next year. You tell your manager about how promising Susan looks and how confident you are about closing her next year.

Was this a good strategy? Maybe, maybe not. What if Susan's current vendor is planning the same enhancement for next year? When they release it, what do you think your chances are then? I will tell you: Zero! What could you have done differently?

When you told Susan about the timeframe for the enhancement, get her fully engaged right then and there. How? By asking if she would assist your product development team in designing the functionality she needs or otherwise participating with other prospects or customers in other aspects of the upgrade, including special features, look-and-feel of the screens (GUI), etc.

More than likely, her current vendor won't ask her for input on this and she could find your interest in her feedback and opinions pretty exciting and enticing. If Susan says yes, and agrees to further engage with you and others at your company, then you truly have just gained access. Congratulations!

CONCLUSION

Gaining access is the first step in any sale. Yes, it's sometimes the most difficult step. But if you're persistent and creative in your approach, you will be successful. Make yourself different, and show prospects that you have the expertise that will help them. This is imperative.

Remember, your approach always changes but your process never does.

Chapter 2:
DETERMINE NEEDS

> " Recognizing the need is the primary condition for design.
>
> — Charles Eames (1907-1978)
> Industrial Designer "

In the previous chapter, Gain Access, we discussed the importance of having prospects talk about themselves, what they do and how they do it. That leads us to this next critical stage. Recognizing needs sets up everything else as you move forward in the sales process. Without proper and accurate needs analysis, you won't be successful.

If you are fortunate enough to have a sales engineer or a solution architect - someone other than yourself who will actually be doing the presentation - then you should have that person join you for a conference call/ web meeting prior to your presentation.

Earlier I talked about the importance of knowing what it is that we are selling. I said the answer that most reps give me is "efficiency," "productivity" or, what one manager once answered, "a good night's sleep." This latter is a truly unique answer for sure. While these are all probably true, in my mind what we actually sell - and everyone sells - is CHANGE.

Mind you, no one likes to change; we are all creatures of habit. We like doing the same things the same way over and over again. We get up at the same time each day, we eat our meals about the same time each day, we work out each day at the same time. We live and breathe on a somewhat fixed schedule. We do this because we find it comfortable and easy. Things have been working fine for me so why do I need to do things differently? If it ain't broke, why fix it?

Resistance to change is not only something sales reps need to recognize in themselves, we need to be aware of this in our prospects, as well. To convert a prospect to a customer, you must prepare them to change. And in order for them to change, you must recognize their needs.

Even if your solution is the best thing out there, sometimes prospects won't buy just because they don't want to change. They will rarely admit this to you, though. Instead they will tell you they don't have the budget, don't see the need, it wasn't approved by upper management, or the dreaded "We have decided to go a different route."

Ugh… that hurts. So let's fix it.

THE PRE-DEMO DISCOVERY CALL

Once sales reps have gained access to a prospect, they jump right into the presentation. They either do the demo themselves or they have their sales assistant or product specialist do the demo. They either go onsite to the prospect's office or do the presentation over the web using tools like Webex, Zoom or GoToMeeting.

Typically, the presentation begins with a PowerPoint that tells the prospect all about the company: they have been in the business for over fifty years, their product or service is an industry leader, they have clients around the world… blah blah blah. Does this sound like you?

If you were lucky enough to get in front of a VP or other key decision-maker, in the thirty minutes you spent justifying your existence, he or she probably left the room, or started checking email, or are now on the phone. Why? Because you brought absolutely no value to them – you put them to sleep. You never talked about their company, their processes, their needs. You didn't set the stage on how you are going to address the problems and concerns that they are facing.

So prior to the presentation, you must engage the prospect, usually on the phone, to determine exactly what his or her needs are. This stage in recognizing their needs is totally about the prospect. The information you gather from this pre-demo call is precisely upon which you are going to base your presentation.

I learned this lesson early on in my career. I knew my product (in this case, software) inside and out; I could do a presentation better than any product specialist. I knew what would sell and what wouldn't. Does this sound like you? I did an outstanding job of showing our software to a top prospect and was wrapping up the demo by saying this is why our customers buy our product.

The prospect then said to me, "That's great to hear why other companies buy from you, but what you showed doesn't help us. So I guess we won't be moving forward." This totally set me back. I then stammered, "What exactly would help you?" and the prospect went on to explain what they were hoping to see based on their unique needs. I wasted hours of their time and mine showing them something they didn't need nor want.

I didn't show them what they wanted because, due to my lack of experience, it wasn't important to me. I assumed it wasn't important to them either. Well, you know what happens when one assumes. Exactly -- the prospect thanked me and hung up.

It took me years before I was able to get back in there but I learned a valuable lesson. Just because I think something is slick or cool in my product, it doesn't mean a prospect will think it's important and relevant. Had I recognized their unique needs, this never would have happened.

Recognizing needs is about asking questions: How do you operate your business or division today? How long have you been doing it this way? What do you like about how you do things? What could be improved in your mind? If you had to create our product (in my case, software) from scratch, what would you want it to do? How would you like it to operate? What are some other products or services with which you would like to integrate it?

I could go on and on with more questions that will help you frame a presentation geared to your prospects as opposed to a generic flavor-of-the-month that many of your competitors present. In fact, if you can get them to provide you with a sample file or other materials applicable to your product or service, that would be even more ideal.

So let's dive deeper into recognizing needs.

I mentioned earlier about having a sales specialist, sales engineer, solution architect or other expert participate on your pre-demo call with your prospect. Why is this important? If this person is performing your demo, he or she will hear first-hand what your prospect wants to see. They should ask questions, verify what's important and what's not. We all say things and hear things differently. Having two of you on this pre-demo call helps identify your prospect's needs and ensure there isn't a misinterpretation or miscommunication between you and the prospect. I'm willing to bet your specialists will ask deeper questions, and possibly better ones, than you alone, once they understand what your prospect is looking for.

Depending on what you are selling, a pre-demo recognized need call could take from 15 minutes up to an hour or longer. The more information you can gather from your prospect, the more compelling your presentation will be. The more compelling, the better your chances of keeping that VP in the room and engaged. Remember, don't spend 30 minutes of your opening getting them bored about your company.

Trash your marketing materials! Sorry, marketing. Your presentation is about them, your prospects – not about you and your company. At this point, your prospect probably already has read everything about you that's on the web or you wouldn't be there.

OK, so you spent time with your prospect in pre-demo discovery. Now what? On to the presentation? Maybe, maybe not. Depending on your product, your sales cycle, the dollar amount of your sale or even the buying process of your customer, it could be the perfect time to create a solution blueprint with your prospect's key buyer.

THE SOLUTION BLUEPRINT

If you are selling to a Fortune 500 company or any large entity, you typically will have to do more than one presentation. During your pre-demo call, or even afterward, get with your key buyer and create a blueprint describing their internal sales processes: How many levels up do they have to go? Is procurement involved? Always? Or only at certain dollar amounts? Does IT or other divisions get involved? If so, when? What are their typical questions/concerns? Is this budgeted and, if not, can they still purchase the program or does it have to wait till next year? Who makes the ultimate decision? Will this person be in the presentation? When can I meet with him/her?

FORECASTING SALES

Knowing the answers to these and other questions early in the sales process will also help you become a better forecaster of your sales. Management cares about forecasting. You may not know or care but, trust me, your management does, especially if you're a public company and shareholders have expectations set by the board of directors. They don't want to let Wall Street have the opinion that they will not meet earnings or EBITA (earnings before income taxes and amortization).

Besides, providing management with periodic sales forecasts will show management you know more than any other sales reps about the deals in progress.

BACK TO THE SOLUTION BLUEPRINT

Create the solution blueprint, then ask your key buyer to review it and make any changes to it. Sometimes he or she won't even want to look at it, let alone review it. But if the key buyer truly believes in you and your product, you may be pleasantly surprised by the feedback. Another one of my favorite expressions is "It never hurts to ask." What's the worst that can happen? They say no. OK, so they said no. This could be a sign to you that maybe the buyer isn't as bought in as you thought; or maybe they just don't want to do it, which is fine. Either way, it's up to you to make that determination, and proceed accordingly.

THE SUCCESS CHECKLIST

So you engaged the prospect during one or more pre-demo discovery calls and created and shared your solutions blueprint. Now let's create a checklist for success. This document is a summary of all the buyer's recognized needs you, alone or with others on your team, garnered. Consider it a living, breathing document, one that will be constantly updated and tracked until closing the sale.

Provide the success checklist to your prospect prior to the presentation. Summarize it first in an email: thank them for their time in reviewing their requirements with you, then list below the data points you heard. Ask if this covers everything we talked about. Ask if there are any other things we need to cover or other departments that could be using the product or service with whom you need to speak. Present this in outline form, make it short and easy for your prospect to fully understand.

Ask yourself if you demonstrate all these answers to their needs during your demo, is it compelling enough for them to make a change? Remember what I said earlier: Change is painful, no one wants to do it .

So if what you see on this checklist is not compelling, you need to do a lot of selling during the presentation to make it compelling. This is when being honest with yourself is more important than anything else. Be objective, be insightful. Does this make sense for them to take on? If you think not, you may need to go back to their recognized needs and dig deeper by asking different questions. It's better to do this now, prior to the presentation, as opposed to wasting your time going down a road that leads to failure.

Remember, you won't be able to justify the price of your product or service if the needs you're solving aren't your buyer's highest priorities.

NOW WHAT – NO FINAL PRESENTATION?

OK, you recognized the needs of your prospect and you're ready for the presentation. You put a closing date 30 days out and you're already counting your commission. Sorry, you already spent your commission. Ready to rock and roll, right? Hate to tell you, but you are in for a rude awakening.

You did everything you're supposed to do. You didn't skip any steps, didn't get way ahead of your prospect. You prepared the solutions blueprint and success checklist. But the key buyer is still stuck on "Why change?" And so you don't get to the presentation. What happened?

So many different things could go wrong, yet none of them could be your fault or the fault of your stakeholder.

One of my top sales reps, Bart, always told me that even as he got closer to signing a contract, the deal was still 50/50. Why was it always 50/50? Because anything unforeseen can happen. Possibly a death, a hurricane. A corporate reorganization. Did your key buyer get turned down by his or her superior? Did he or she get fired? Does the company have no interest in changing? Did the company just get sold with a freeze on new purchases?

No matter how well you did everything up to now, you just have no definitive foreknowledge or control of what ultimately will happen. Bart also would tell me that even after he had the signed contract, it was still 50/50. Seriously? Why is that? Because sometimes what could go wrong does go wrong.

LAST MINUTE SURPRISES

Fortunately, there are some steps you can take to mitigate against such unforeseen events. Sales reps often rely on only one buyer or internal champion. But as you are going through the recognize needs stage, find out who else is involved in the decision making process. Begin to build a relationship with that person. Get them on your team as an advocate for you.

If possible, involve more personnel from your sales team. The more momentum you build, the more you can anticipate possible roadblocks looming ahead and the more likely you will execute the final sales presentation.

CONCLUSION

If you recognize your prospects' true needs upfront and get sample data from them, you have a much stronger chance of executing the final sales presentation. Customizing your presentation with their data and showing them how your product or service will meet their needs if they purchased your product or service is so incredibly valuable, it amazes me why every sales person doesn't do it. And why is that? Probably because it takes time, it takes persistence, it takes dedication. And quite honestly, many of you don't have it!

Did I hit a nerve? Good. Perhaps it's time to make those changes I addressed at the top of this chapter.

Chapter 3:
THE PRESENTATION

> During the first few minutes of your presentation, your job is to assure the audience members that you are not going to waste their time and attention.
>
> — Dale Ludwig
> Sales Coach and Trainer

You gained access, you did your pre-demo discovery. It's finally up to you, your product expert and maybe your manager to show your prospects why your product or service is the best of the best to meet and exceed their needs. Now it's time to execute the presentation.

What are your roles, who does what, how do you start, how do you end and what happens in between all of this?

It's show time. You're now on stage. This is your presentation. Not the sales engineer's nor that of any other member of the sales team. It's yours and yours alone. I have experienced way too many times when a sales engineer would take control, do and say whatever he or she wants, and completely forget about the pre-demo call with the prospect, their recognized needs, the blueprint and checklist. Wind them up and off they go. Many might be on their fourth demo of the day. Engineers don't get mad at me for saying this. I started my career as a sales engineer so you know what I'm saying contains more than a modicum of truth.

 ## AVOID TOO MUCH DETAIL

Most presentations I've witnessed go into way too much detail. Product people are very proud of their creations. They want to show off all the bells and whistles instead of focusing on what the prospect wants and needs or what the sales rep told them to present. The presentation becomes more of a training class versus a presentation.

If the prospect asks a question about capability, the product person says "Yes, we can do that" and then spends the next twenty minutes showing it when all the prospect wanted was a yes or no answer.

It would help tremendously if a sales engineer simply can answer with a "Yes, we can do that, do I need to show it to you?" Most times the prospect will answer no. If they do say yes, then the sales engineer should respect the time that is remaining and say something like, "We have x minutes remaining, I can show you how to do that now but we won't be able to cover some other capabilities you said were important. How would you like me to proceed? Now, or we can schedule a demo of that for another time. What would you like me to do?"

ROLES AND RESPONSIBILITIES

Let's get back to roles and responsibilities for a few minutes. You're the sales representative. You're in control. It's your sale to win or lose. I hate it when a sales rep introduces himself/herself and basically says "Here's Johnny!" Seriously, you can and should do better.

It's your job to manage and even control the presentation. You and the engineer should be on the conference line at least 5 minutes before start time. You should make sure the Webex or other conference program you are using is working and you're logged in. Review the materials that are going to be presented. The product person prior to getting on the stage or web platform should confirm again that all programs are operational and the functionality that is going to be presented is working.

As your prospects join the meeting or call, introduce yourself and welcome them. Then verify they can see whatever is displayed.

One of the training classes I took a couple of years ago was Demo to Win from a company based in Colorado Springs. The training was excellent and if you as a sales engineer are ever able to take this class it would help you tremendously. But I will tell you that you need to be open to changing how you present and your company must fully support this methodology as even the sales reps need to beware of it and in sync with this new style.

The concept is simple: Open with a limbic. (Don't know what a limbic opening is? I will explain shortly). Then tell them what they are going to see, show it to them, tell them again what they saw. People begin to remember things when they hear it three or more times.

Let's dive into this a little more deeply.

LIMBIC OPENINGS

Limbic openings provide an analogy of your product. It sets the scene for the presentation. For example, I often show a picture of an iceberg and say something like, "Most people in their jobs have visibility to see solely what they are responsible for and can make decisions based only on what they see. The problem is that when something unexpected arises, they need to decide if they should change course. Is it safe for them to move left or right? Unfortunately, they don't have visibility as to how big the iceberg is because they don't have all the data or information.

Then I show a second picture of what's hidden under the water and how far and wide the iceberg truly is. I continue on: "What our software does for your company is reveal the holistic view of your organization vs just a silo view. This is what we are going to show you today."

Start your presentation like that vs what you're probably doing today which is: "Hello, my name is Jeff Brandeis and today my team is going to show you how you will make better, smarter decisions than ever before." Which opening do you think will get their attention faster and retain it longer? Which do you think that executive, that key decision-maker will be more compelled to stay and watch?

This is about doing things differently. This is what you as the sales rep should be doing. Setting the stage up front before even introducing yourself and who from your team is on the phone. Be different from your competitors. This will help set you apart.

Want them to remember your presentation? Then make it memorable.

FUNDAMENTAL SKILLS

At this point, introduce yourself and whomever else is on the phone or in the room from your company.

No, it's not time for you to do the hand-off to your product person quite yet. It's time for you to set the agenda.

Summarize from the solution blueprint that you created (see Chapter 2) what was discussed with your key buyers. Ask if there is anything else that is of importance to anyone that was not listed. It's a great question as you may not know everyone in the room or on the call and you have no idea what their objective or role is by attending the presentation.

This sets the stage.

So what happens if you get more items? First thing you do is thank the person for bringing up the topic and make sure you write it down in your notes. If you know that the topic will be covered, respond by saying, "John will be showing that to you about x way through the presentation." If you really want to score some big points later when Susan is about to cover that topic, speak up and say something like, "Excuse me, John, but during our opening, I believe it was Paul that asked the question about x and Susan is about to show it to him."

This is a great technique. You acknowledged Paul when you remembered his question and showed further interest in letting him know it's about to get shown. Typically, Susan will answer Paul's question and continue on. But don't stop there.

Ask Paul if Susan answered his question. By doing so, you won another point. You are verifying that what was shown was answered well and finding out if Paul was or was not totally satisfied with the answer. Then ask him if he has any other questions or concerns. Just make sure he doesn't dwell on something that could be a negative and ultimately hurt your chances of a sale.

It is also possible that you might need to get back with Paul at a later time to dive deeper into his question. Again, ask the buyer's team if this is an area a major concern for everyone or is this an area that only Paul specializes in? This will tell you how big of an issue or concern this really is.

I have seen situations when the sales engineer gets upset when the sales rep interrupts. It slows them down, they say. They lose momentum, they are revved up and on a mission. But, again, you're the captain. You need to manage the presentation.

It's up to you to control the tempo, the pace, ask if there are questions or even come up with benefit statements on what was just shown if it solves a problem that was discussed earlier. Work with your presenters; they should know in advance when you are going to say something. Teamwork here will help you both. When the sales rep speaks it gives the other presenters a few minutes to think about what's coming up, look at the time, listen to the prospect before restarting.

Your presentation needs to flow like a powerful movie or book, so follow the tell-show-tell format. You and your team need to break up the presentation into chapters. And for each chapter, tell the buyers what they will see demonstrated, perform the demo, then tell again. Keep it simple.

Getting into the weeds, especially on a first demo, will most likely hurt your chances of moving along and getting to the next stage of the sales process.

One other thing that I believe will make your presentation stand out vs the competition. It's a big one for both you and your engineer to do and get used to doing. And that is to deploy video or a webcam. No, I am not suggesting you use camera for the entire presentation. But why not turn it on while the attendees are joining the presentation? Let them put a face to your name, to your company. Reps have told me they don't want prospects to see them, their offices or -- with many of you working at home -- to see that you are working out of your basement that only has studs and no walls or sheet rock. Or reps tells me that means they would have to get dressed and out of their pajamas. Oh my!

Seriously, this is your livelihood we're talking about. Your profession. It's easy to change the background of your office by putting up a dark drop cloth or purchasing a folding paneling that you can put right behind you. So you have to get dressed? Get over it! You might even have to shower and shave! So what? And you may even have to put on a suit and tie, depending on what your selling and who your buyer is. Turn the camera on and even keep it on during the limbic opening. Once the product presentation starts, turn them all off. Also mute your phone if you have dogs or kids at home. Less noise during the presentation the better. It's time to focus and listen..

When the presentation is over and it's time to wrap things up, summarize on a slide the key points that were covered. Turn the camera back on and get out of your comfort zone. You need to do things differently than the way your competitor is doing. They need to remember you, they need to remember your product. This will help tremendously in having them achieve just that.

THE DO-NOTS

Let's talk a little more about the do-nots of the presentation as I already have covered the to-dos.

Don't spend 30 minutes telling them about your company or the history of it and how great your software or other product or service is, nor how your company provides world class support. Boooriiing! The VP or other key decision make will leave within 5 minutes if you do this.

As I said in previous chapter, they did their research, they know you, they also know your competitors. Spend the time you have with them wisely.

What they want to know is WIIFM aka "What's in it for me?"

Don't spend time reciting your resume, or that of your engineer's. Hopefully both of you know your stuff and it will come through loud and clear during the presentation.. The time you have for your presentation is valuable. Use it wisely.

Sales engineers: You don't need to explain every box, every line of code, every form or section. Show them what they really need to see and nothing more. Sorry to tell you this, but somebody has to. Might as well be me.

Also many of you tend to make your product more difficult to use as you jump up and down the screens. Speak slowly and concisely. One of my pet peeves during presentations is what I call the live mouse syndrome. You love moving the mouse around the screen. You love drawing circles with your mouse, you move it left, you move it right, you move up, you move it down. You do the mouse dance. No offense but this is distracting, it's annoying and you are just confusing your participants.

"Wow," you say, "seriously, Jeff. I've been doing this job for years and no one ever told me this, it's not a big deal." Let me tell you, sir or ma'am. It is.

No one has told you because they were afraid to tell you or didn't know how to tell you. Get to the section of your product you want to talk about. Put the mouse there and take your hand off the mouse. Leave it alone. Separating from your mouse will be difficult for you because you have been doing this for so long.

Sales reps: Copy and paste this section into an email and send it to your engineer. My guess is they aren't even aware they are doing this.

Sales engineers: Have you ever recorded your own presentation and tried to critique yourself objectively? Try it. If I were your manager, I would insist you do this. Sales reps won't tell you this because they need you for their next demo and don't want to rock the boat.

AVOID PRODUCT DUMPS

OK, let's go back to the don'ts. Don't do what is called the "product dump". Present what is supposed to be presented and stay away from going into areas about which the prospect hasn't asked nor really cares. If you and your team did the pre-demo call correctly, then your blueprint or game plan was done for you. What you need to do is stay on track, stay on course.

MORE DO-NOTS TO CONSIDER

A word of caution: Don't use a lot of humor or tell many jokes during your presentation. What you think is funny, others may not; what you think is cute, again, others may not. The last thing you want to do is offend someone. What you should do is tell a story here and there – a story around clients using your product and how it was beneficial to them. How a company similar to your prospect solved a problem by using your product in this manner.

Stories are great if you can weave them into your presentation. Especially if it's a personal story. Your authenticity will be reflected in changes in your delivery. Your audience will sense that and become even more engaged. This is how you build your credibility. Story-telling is one of the most successful sales techniques you can use. They are powerful.

Sales engineer: Call your existing clients, talk to them about what they do and how they use your product.

 *There's an old joke that goes like this: "What is the best way to get to Carnegie Hall? Practice! Practice! Practice!" How do you stop these little annoying habits? Practice! Practice! Practice!*

How much time has it saved them? I bet many of your customers use your product in unique ways, oftentimes different than how you intended it to be used. Learn from this and put your findings into your presentation. "That's a really great question." Have you ever heard presenters use that expression? Sometimes they say it several times in a row, trying to make the people who asked the question feel good.

But what happens when you get a question and don't say that it's a really great question? That person you failed to compliment has probably mentally checked out of your presentation because he/she did not get a compliment. Silly, you think, but trust me -- they did and do.

You're probably thinking I'm knit-picking and in some ways I am. While you're on stage, you are performing and your audience is watching every move you make. They are listening to every word. Any little slips and blunders tend to grow and become bigger and bigger the more you do it. It's like an open wound: the more you pick at it, the bigger it gets. What's worse is you don't even know you' re doing it. How do you stop?

Just as I advised sales engineers earlier, sales reps – indeed, every member of the sales team – should record at least one of their presentations. Then listen and watch intently. Next, mute the sound and watch it again. Do you constantly move the mouse? Do you scroll through screens quickly? Do you smile and appear to be enjoying the demo? Perhaps one of the things most presenters forget is that there is a slight time lag between what you are seeing vs what your audience is seeing. Sometimes it's a few seconds, sometimes longer. Pace your presentation accordingly.

As a sales rep, you may be thinking all these issues don't concern you. If that's the case, you'd be dead wrong. It concerns you big-time, more than you could imagine. Remember, you are the captain of this presentation. You are supposed to control it, steer it and make sure it goes the way you planned it. Don't let a mutiny happen, even unconsciously, by an engineer. You don't want to crash into that iceberg, do you?

REMOTE VERSUS ONSITE PRESENTATIONS

Remote presentations are becoming much more common than being physically in front of your prospect. Being onsite is still the best way to present in my mind. Many of the dos and don'ts I described above apply whether you're on remote or onsite.

Onsite obviously provides you the ability to meet your prospect face-to-face. You can see if they are engaged or not. You can interact with them, as well.

Where do you set up? Where do you sit? Where does the principal presenter sit? My preference is that the presenter sit in the front where he/she is looking or facing the audience. Too often I see the engineer sitting in the back. More importantly, all members of the sales team stand, not sit, when addressing the prospects. In fact, should you stand for the entire presentation? Yes!

Standing up while presenting provides you a more powerful command of the room. You can observe more, you can interact better and, most importantly, your voice tones command more authority when standing vs. sitting.

To avoid bending over to move your mouse and see your screen, invest in a portable computer presentation desk that you can buy for under $50.

So now you are on site and you have remote attendees, as well. Get there early, verify that everything is operational, such as Internet access and the ability of remote attendees to log into your presentation. Make sure you have a back-up plan, just in case. Have an offline PowerPoint of your entire presentation ready to go, including all screen shots from the beginning to the end of your presentation. But, Jeff, this could take hours if not days to prepare. Yes, it could. But what's the cost if you have a full room of people and you can't access your presentation materials?

This actually happened to me earlier in my career. We were selling a new software product to over 50 different government agencies. Two full hours were allocated to our presentation. A priceless opportunity. You don't get 50 government agencies together in one location very often. I opened the presentation providing them a high level overview of what they were going to see, used my iceberg story as my limbic opening. I had their attention. They were ready to see the software. Then I handed it off to our product specialist who was remote and located in India. He started his presentation.

Five minutes into the demo we lost him. Lost the voice, lost the Webex, lost everything. Our company president was on the phone, as well. How embarrassing! She couldn't log into his demo environment, we had no backup slides, no screen shots. We were screwed. I wound up turning the next two hours into a question and answer session. I got the audience involved with asking what they saw as their biggest challenges. What they were hoping to learn from us. But we couldn't show them anything.

I was the only one onsite and walked out feeling deflated and miserable. Here was an opportunity we just blew as we didn't have a backup plan. Afterwards, I tried to re-engage with many of the agencies but I got no response. They eliminated us because we failed at the presentation. Who could blame them? I would do the same. All because we didn't have a backup plan.

I should have known better. But I've learned from that bitter lesson – and now so have you!

FOLLOW-UP QUESTIONS

As the sales rep, you stand up and go to the front of the room (if you are not there already). Start with your limbic opening and you're off and running till the first question comes up. You, your sales engineer or other sales team member answers it and you continue on. Right? Wrong.

First thing every presenter should do during a presentation is repeat the question. Make sure you truly understand it. And secondly, by repeating the question, the people on the phone (if remote) or at the back of the room (if onsite) can hear it loud and clear. This is a great habit to get into and one that also requires discipline.

In addition, by repeating the question, it provides you or your team a few additional seconds to think of an answer. Sometimes, even if you're prepared to answer the question at that moment, you might wish to park the question or put it to the side for now. You do this by saying something like, "Paul, do you mind if I answer that question a bit later?" Paul should say, "Sure that's fine," but be certain you don't forget about it or Paul won't be a happy prospect.

The sales rep is also responsible for taking notes of what they like, what answers maybe they didn't like, what the follow-up items might be, etc. The sales engineer can't be doing all this while presenting. This is your job. As a former boss of mine used to tell me, "Don't screw it up!" Well, he used different words but you get the idea.

Following up on these items is imperative. It shows your interest in the prospect, it shows your attentive to them. But most of all, it shows them you want their business. If you don't follow up, you won't get the business.

A great practice – no pun intended - is to email your key buyer the questions you gathered along with each person's name who asked the question. Request the email and phone numbers of those persons and send the answers to those questions directly to that individual. Make sure there isn't a follow up question, as well. This is your job as sales representative. Getting answers and doing the follow-up. Don't expect your engineer to do this. Their job is to do the presentation. They can't be presenter, note taker and follow-up person while you're checking your email and not paying attention. No matter how good your engineer, only you manage the sales process and this is part of your process.

POST-PRESENTATION REVIEW

One year at our annual kick-off meeting; our executive team brought in pilots from the Blue Angels. What do pilots have to do with sales? It's about teamwork and coordination. Relying on one another to do the right thing.

In the air, a single mistake could mean the life or death of the pilot and crew, and those on the ground. In a sales environment, it could mean the life or death of your sale. The point I'm driving at is this: After each flight, the Blue Angels flight crew sit down and discuss the good, the bad and the ugly of the flight. Rank and tenure go out the window. It's a nameless, rank-less environment. Most importantly, and the most difficult for them to do, is leaving their egos at the door. When it's life and death situations, egos can't get in the way.

Same thing in sales.

After each presentation, the entire sales team in attendance from your company should do a debrief. This isn't about name-calling or making someone feel terrible. It's about critiquing the presentation, how the team can do better. What did they like, what didn't go well, could we have done something different? It's not what you say, it's how you say it. This is a very hard concept but one that can be beneficial to everyone if handled professionally.

This is why post-presentation feedback is essential. Comments from nameless and rankless colleagues are key to driving sales. It's in the best interest of the entire team to do this. If everyone truly wants to get better, this is a mandatory step.

If you don't think any of what I have pointed out is important, then why are you still reading? Did I hit a nerve? I hope I did.

CONCLUSION

Executing a compelling and effective presentation will take time to master. There is quite a bit for both you and your team to learn. It requires overcoming many challenges. But if you can work through them -- through Practice! Practice! Practice! -- your chances for success will increase.

And success means more sales, which means more money for you and your team in the end.

Chapter 4:
ALIGN WITH BUYER

> When in doubt, check if your actions are aligned with your purpose.
>
> — Azim Jamal & Brian Tracy
> Executive Coaches

OK. You did your presentation and everyone on your team believes they nailed it and there is no way you don't get this contract. You're high-fiving, you text your boss that it went great.

Two weeks later you get the news -- you lost the sale. What happened?

You are no different than most sales reps. You likely skipped steps in the sales process. Perhaps you emailed your key buyer, thanked him or her for coordinating the presentation, asked if there were any follow up questions. You even might have emailed your contact the answers to your open questions. So what went wrong?

You failed to align with your prospect.

You lost touch, you lost momentum. You started celebrating and thinking about the commission you just earned. So, again, what went wrong?

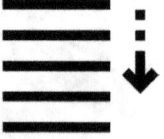 ## HOW TO GAIN ALIGNMENT

You didn't circle back with the key players or decision-makers and ask for their feedback to the presentation. What they liked, what they didn't like. What questions came up after they met as a team? If you truly had the guts, you should ask, "What did my competitors do that I didn't do?" Most of you are too afraid to ask this, or never even thought of asking this question. Why the heck not? It's one of the most telling questions. Helps you to find out who you are competing against, what features they are showing that you didn't, what needs you failed to recognize and other possible deal-breakers.

This is called aligning with your prospect.

You can't close until you align with them. Did you answer all the questions? Are all the objections handled? Did we cover everything? Is price an objection? Is the implementation time frame a problem? Are they truly ready to buy? Ready to sign? Do you even know what their internal process is for signature? Is there a legal review? Wow, you never thought of these things. Well, you should have if you've been reading this book carefully.

I find sales reps often are way ahead of their prospects in the sales cycle because your prospect has a buying process that you never asked about. Oh my!

To align with your prospect, you now need to get in sync with how your prospect buys -- not how you want to sell. There is a big difference here. This is also why most reps do a crappy job at forecasting. You don't understand your buyers. Even worse if you get handed off to a purchasing or legal review.

You think they buy on your timeline. Well, better to learn this now rather than later: They don't.

Incentives might help, but many buyers believe that more and better incentives will become available if they play hard-to-get.

So let's pretend you do have the inside track on the

sale but your prospect has some objections. Could be price, could be capability, could be internal resistance, as well. What do you do?

Most of you start with price. Your prospect says your price is higher than your competition. You probably ask, "How much higher is it?" They might tell you or they might not. What do you do next? You probably ask, "Well, if I get you a discount, or a bigger discount, would you buy?" They answer that it would help. So you thank them and say you'll get back to them soon.

A day or so passes. You provide them another discount. They say thank-you and they will get back with you.
If you did that you're a fool. Why? What did you get in return? Nothing! Aligning is a negotiation. If you give something, you need to get something. They got a discount; you got nothing. What you also neglected to ask – and, again, this is a sin of most reps: "Besides prices, are there any other objections or concerns that would prevent the sale from closing?

Wow, now that's a powerful question! You ask this question and now you need to shut up. If you talk first, you're dead.

 **SILENCE IS GOLDEN**

Silence is a very powerful negotiation technique. Yes, I say "technique" because that's what it is. Most of you don't know when to shut up and be quiet. Sales is also a game. At this stage of the game, after the presentation, the one who talks first loses. Meaning, if you talk after asking a powerful question, you won't get an answer to your question. If they talk first, they typically will feel the urge to answer your question, which is exactly what you want them to do.

Never give a concession until you truly understand the entire picture. Once you understand what you are up against in its entirety, you will know how to react to the situation.

AVOID PRICING SURPRISES

I have always sold products that cost more than those of my competitors. So I typically tell my prospect sometime before I provide pricing that I am priced higher than the others. Why? It sets their expectation and eliminates sticker shock.

When price does come up as an objection as I align us for the close, I remind my prospect of what I initially told them up front. Then I ask, "Besides price, are there any other objections as to why we would not be moving forward with a contract?"

Again, there's that powerful question. And once again, ask it and shut up. Let them answer.

Once you hear their objections, you can proceed to overcome, mitigate and eliminate them. Confirm there aren't any other objections before circling back to price. I'm convinced your key players and proponents must be completely aligned on pricing concerns. If they aren't, you're in trouble. Circling back to the buyer, I would say, "You mentioned to me that the cost of our product was higher than our competitors'. I am not surprised, there are several reasons for that. One of our competitors has not included everything that our product does now and will do in the future."

This is when you must know everything about your product and specifically how it fares much better than those of your competitors. You must be able to rattle off three key differentiators that truly sets your product apart from your competition. Without this knowledge, you will lose the deal.

These three key differentiators must be of critical importance to your prospect. If not, they become "who cares" items. How do you know if they are important? Refer to your Success Checklist. Review what you found out during your presentation.

Remember tell-show-tell? When you drove home your key differentiators, you gained an agreement with the buyer that these are extremely important to them and likely part of their ROI calculus when buying your product.

This then becomes your punch line, your knockout blows to your competition. You have to re-enforce these blows to truly gain alignment and hopefully make the price no longer a significant objection. If it still is, at least you re-positioned the sale. The buyer now understands your value and it becomes a question of whether or not they see that same value in paying more to get more.

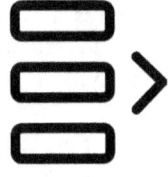 **EXTREME ALIGNMENT**

There will be times when you may be required to go to extreme lengths to successfully gain alignment with a buyer.

Early in my career, I worked for a tax service bureau company. Our customers were CPA firms and accountants. When mainframes were more popular than computers, our customers would complete input sheets that contained all the tax information for their clients. They would then send it to us for processing. We charged them per return. If changes subsequently were made, they were billed for a rerun or a reprocessing fee.

I was selling to a large New York regional accounting firm. After the presentation, they wanted to budget for this cost. Due to rerun charges and other fees that we billed, it was impossible to predict how much any company would pay us. For a CPA firm of this size, it would cost them six figures, just based on their tax return volume.

This was where creativity was needed. Thinking outside the box. This sale would be a huge win for us as they were using our #1 competitor. Coming up with a way to provide them what they wanted and to make this a win for us was going to be difficult. I struggled with what to do for almost two weeks. Then I had a thought.

I asked them what they had in mind for a total cost. They came back with $175,000. The accountant in me then kicked in. I took at a look at all the upstate

New York firms with which we did business as we had billing summaries for each company. I looked at the costs of initial processing and how many times a typical CPA firm did reruns. I arrived at an average price per return, excluding handling fees, shipping etc. I built in a negotiation margin (aka "wiggle room") and presented it to my boss: a fixed fee concept or a site license fee.

The number I arrived at was $275,000 or 100 thousand dollars more than what they told me. My Vice President liked this concept and took it up to the Board, as this was a totally new pricing concept. They approved it and I went back to my prospect.

I showed them in detail how I arrived at the license price, and why it was justified. I also provided them a 3 year term. So now they not only had a predictable fee for year 1, they also could budget for years 2 and 3. We went back and forth on price but settled at $250,000.

We signed a contract and began implementing a brand pricing methodology that the entire industry began to use. I created and sold the first site license contract ever created. I did so in order to align with my prospect on what they wanted by pursuing a creative, and extreme, solution that involved middle and senior management and the Board of Directors.

A total win/win.

CONCLUSION

Objections come in many varieties. Price, term, legal, capabilities and your delivery schedule could be all last minute objections. Some are thrown at you to see how much more the prospect can get from you. Some really matter, some don't. How do you know which is which?

Well… you simply ask.

Ask your prospect to rank them in terms of importance. Ask which objection will prevent them from signing. Most sales people for some strange (i.e.: stupid) reason are afraid to ask tough questions. Or they don't bother with this step and simply provide a contract and expect a signature as if by magic.

Alignment means handling buyer objections and overcoming them. Alignment is paramount to closing the sale. You did the presentation, you handled the questions.

Now comes the make-it-or-break-it part of the sale – the Closing.

Chapter 5:
DONE DEAL!

> **All progress takes place outside the comfort zone.**
>
> — Michael John Bobak
> Artist, Author & Poet

CONGRATULATIONS – FOR NOW

You are now at the last step of the sales process: the close. The famous close. This is sometimes the most terrifying step for many sales reps. Yes, they – you, perhaps? - are actually afraid of the close. Why is that?

You may fear rejection, or simply the word "no." You fear the prospect might tell you your product is not what they selected. Or perhaps you fear the phrase "your price is too high."

So what do you do instead? Sometimes, you may throw a contract over to your prospect via email and ask them to sign and return it. Or you may sit back and send emails asking your prospect for a status of where they are in the decision process. Sometimes you even continue to send your prospects sales literature or testimonials about your product. You continue to sell.

STOP, YOU FOOL!

If you have performed all the other steps correctly, the close should be a natural and easy conversation. Depending on you particular prospect, as you now have aligned yourselves and gained agreement that everything you provided is exactly what they need -- including price, time frames for delivery and implementation, etc. -- then you should ask your prospect, "Is there any reason why you wouldn't sign our agreement to move forward?"

Ask this and then do what?

Nothing! Keep quiet! Remember, if you talk first now, you lose.

SILENCE IS STILL GOLDEN

This is so difficult for some sales people to handle: keeping quiet and remaining silent. You asked the most important question that you can ask. If the prospect doesn't answer with a yes, no or maybe, you lose.

But if you speak first, you most likely will continue to sell; or explain why you are better than the competition; or show why your ROI is higher and better; or talk about additional features of your product. Blah-blah-blah.

What did you just do when you spoke first? You took steps backwards in the sales process rather than. moving it forward.

I stated earlier that one of the biggest mistakes that reps make is that they get ahead of their prospects in the sales cycle. You want the sale fast; your prospect is thinking 3 to 4 months. By speaking first, you just let your prospect off the hook. You had them in your sights, you were about to bring them in and you just provided them a way out. Now they can and will circle back to talk about whatever topic you just brought up.

Sales is a checklist, folks, it's a process. If you speak first, you should, like in the game of Monopoly, go directly to jail, do not pass go and collect $200. By speaking first you probably are going to need to align yourselves again and possibly even worse, do another presentation. Ughh! That is the last thing you want to do.

Silence during a sales call, or a negotiation is one of the most uncomfortable things for both you and your prospect. You are supposed to be a trained professional. You are supposed to handle these types of situations with polish and poise. Don't get nervous, don't get uncomfortable. Let your prospect do that. Let them speak. If you haven't got a DONE DEAL (no pun intended) of going through your earlier steps, you will now find out. Why? Because they either need to sign the contract or tell you why they won't. It's that simple.

 ## POST-SALE ISSUES

Even after the sale closes, things can go wrong: Your software or other product is difficult to install, the training goes poorly, the one person that voted against the purchase now becomes more vocal about change and the learning curve.

Again, there are steps to be taken to mitigate such post-sale failures.

Always stay involved with a sale until they are fully operational. If a sale gets canceled in the first year or the buyer doesn't pay for the purchase, depending on your company policies, you may get charged back for the sale. You basically will owe your company money. Don't become one of those sales reps that build relationships through the sales process, close the sale -- then never again pick up the phone to talk with your client.

Stay involved, remain visible.

CONCLUSION

For sales professionals, closing the sale is a process. You've traveled from gaining access to the pre-demo call. From recognizing needs to the presentation. From alignment to the closing – and beyond.

The steps of this process as outlined in this book will be as effective as the diligence with which you apply them. Sales is an art, but it's also a science. If you follow its laws, which includes many opportunities to think outside-of-the-box, I believe you can achieve a success ranking nothing short of a DONE DEAL!

FINAL THOUGHTS

All of us are in sales. Every time we talk to a customer, prospect - even a friend - we are selling.

If you want to sell more of your products or services, follow the DONE DEAL! process and don't skip steps. Sell based on your prospects needs and time frame.

If you do this, you will sell more.

Good Selling!

Jeff Brandeis

ABOUT THE AUTHOR

For over 25 years, Jeff Brandeis has held various sales positions at regional, national and international firms, from a sales support representative to senior management where he supervised and coached teams of sales representatives and sales engineers.

He began his sales career working for Computer Language Research as a Market Support Representative, moved to Account Representative and was promoted to Division Sales Manager.

Less than a year later, Jeff was recruited by CCH Incorporated, which was subsequently purchased by Wolters Kluwer in Chicago, where he was promoted to Head of Major Accounts. He has held numerous positions at Wolters Kluwer CCH including Vice President of Solution Design, Vice President of Sales – Accounting, and Vice President of Sales for CCH TeamMate.

Prior to entering sales, Jeff worked for 5 years as an accountant at a global accounting firm. He earned his Master's in Taxation from Long Island University's CW Post College and his Bachelor of Business Administration from Baruch College in New York City.

Jeff Brandeis' background working in CPA firms taught him the Power of Process and, as a sales executive, came to discover most sales representatives and companies do not have a great sales process.

He wrote DONE DEAL! to provide you with a simple and proven, easy-to-learn 5-step process which, when followed, will increase sales, generate more profits and lead to a more fulfilling career.

Today, Jeff has joined forces with Paul Webb to operate Done Deal Sales Training. Together Paul and Jeff teach sales people not only the DONE DEAL! sales process but also to understand how people learn, which determines how people will buy.

Visit Donedealsalestraining.com to learn more.

Visit
Done Deal Sales Training

and master the DONE DEAL! ultimate
sales process through accelerated learning.
Over 40,000 students have attended our
courses...find out what they already know
and get started on your path to growth
and great success.

donedealsalestraining.com

NOTES

_____

_____

_____

_____

_____

_____

_____

_____

_____

_____

_____

_____

_____

_____

_____

_____

_____

_____

_____

_____

_____

_____

_____

_____

_____

_____

_____

_____

NOTES

_____
_____
_____
_____
_____
_____
_____
_____
_____
_____
_____
_____
_____
_____
_____
_____
_____
_____
_____
_____
_____
_____
_____
_____

www.ingramcontent.com/pod-product-compliance
Lightning Source LLC
Chambersburg PA
CBHW070505220526
45467CB00002B/580